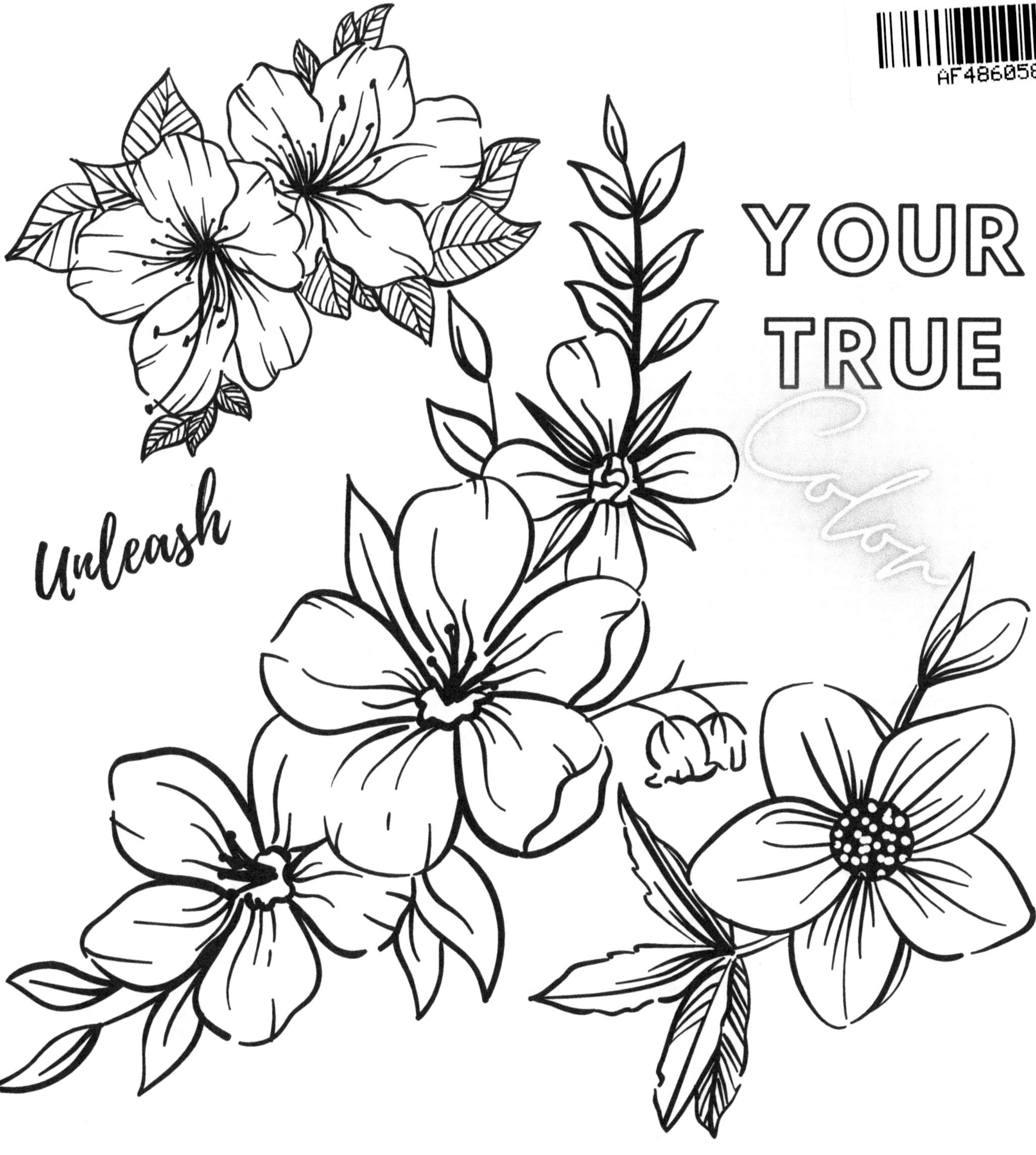

This
coloring book
belongs to

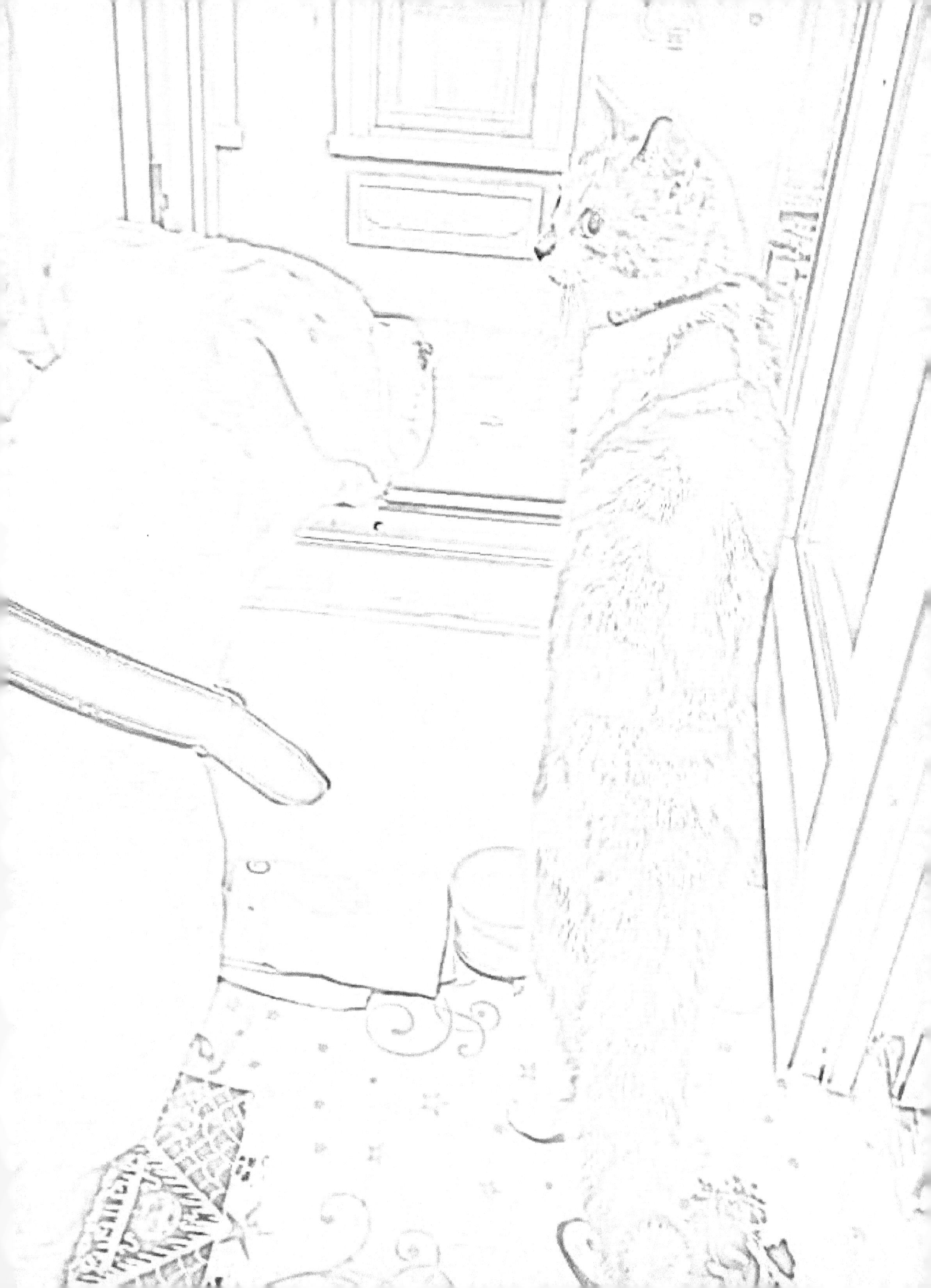

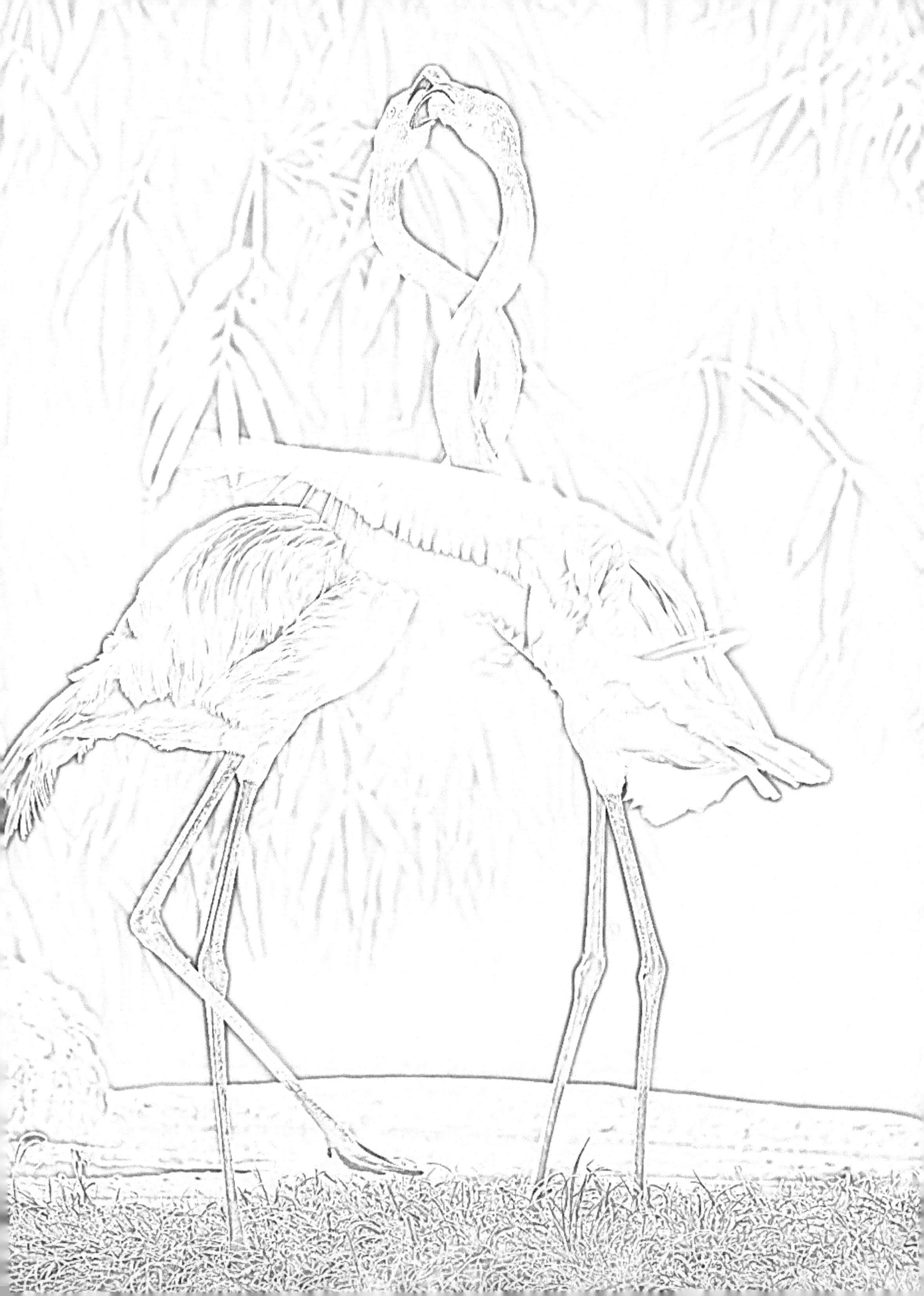

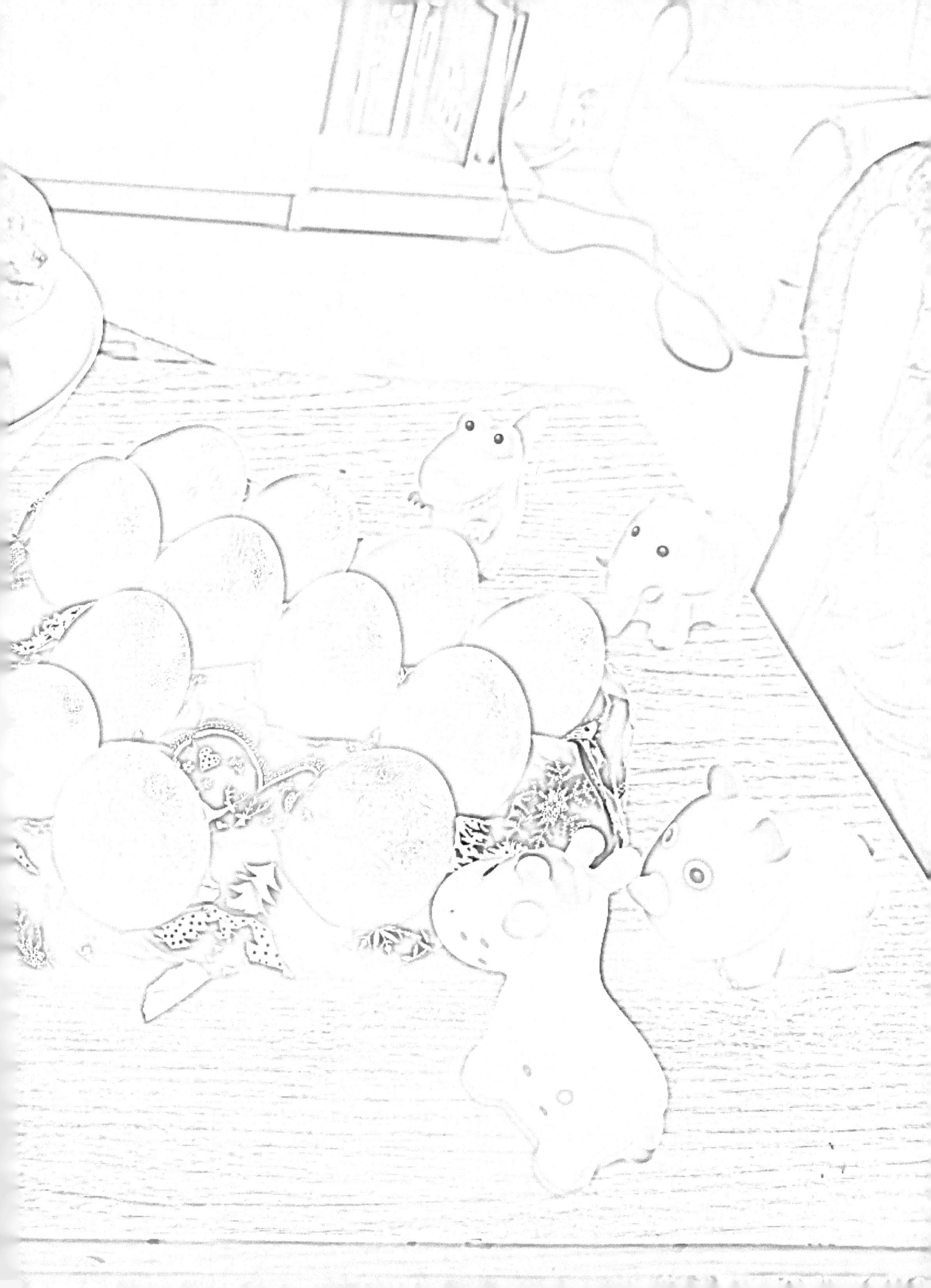

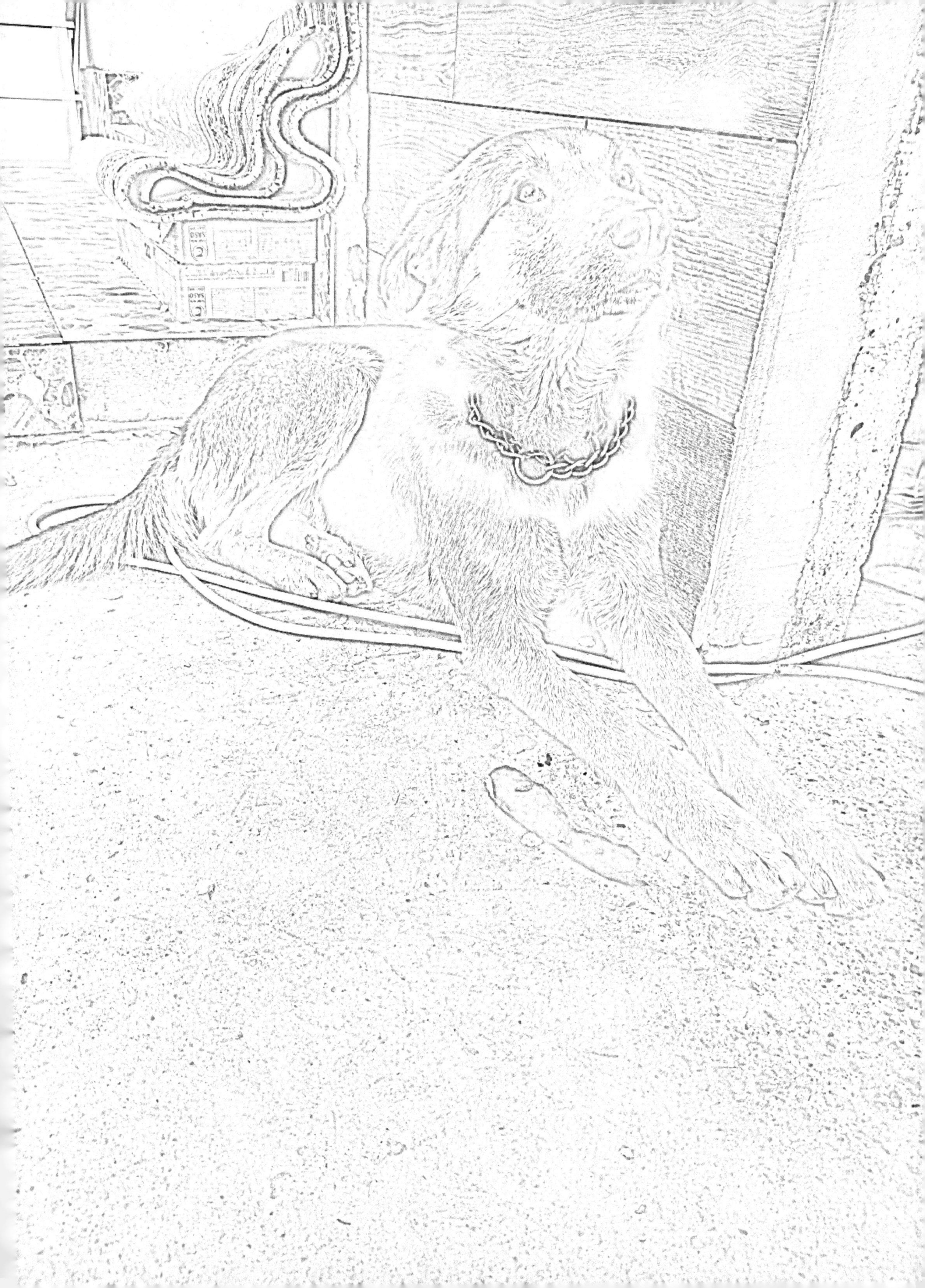

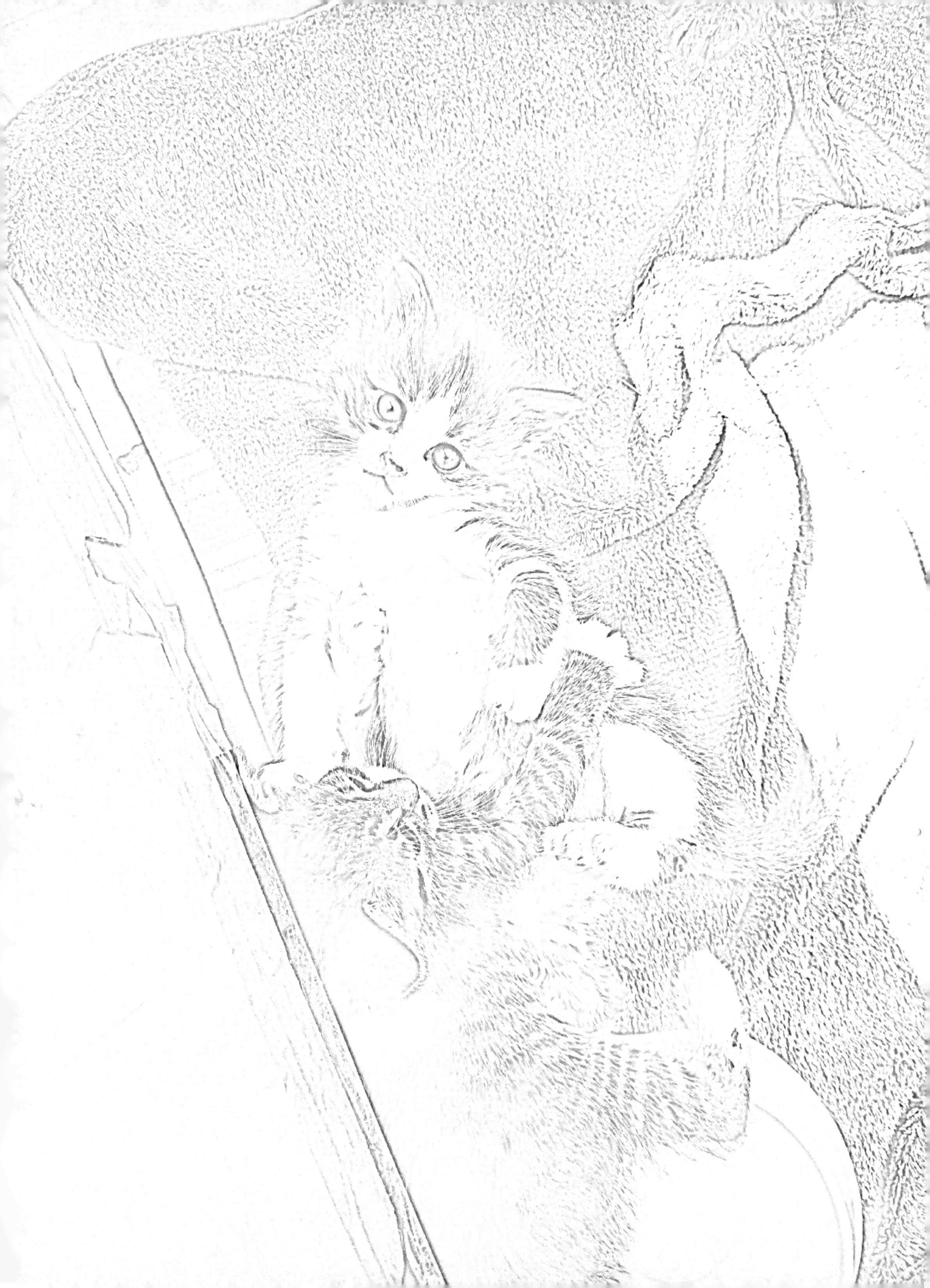

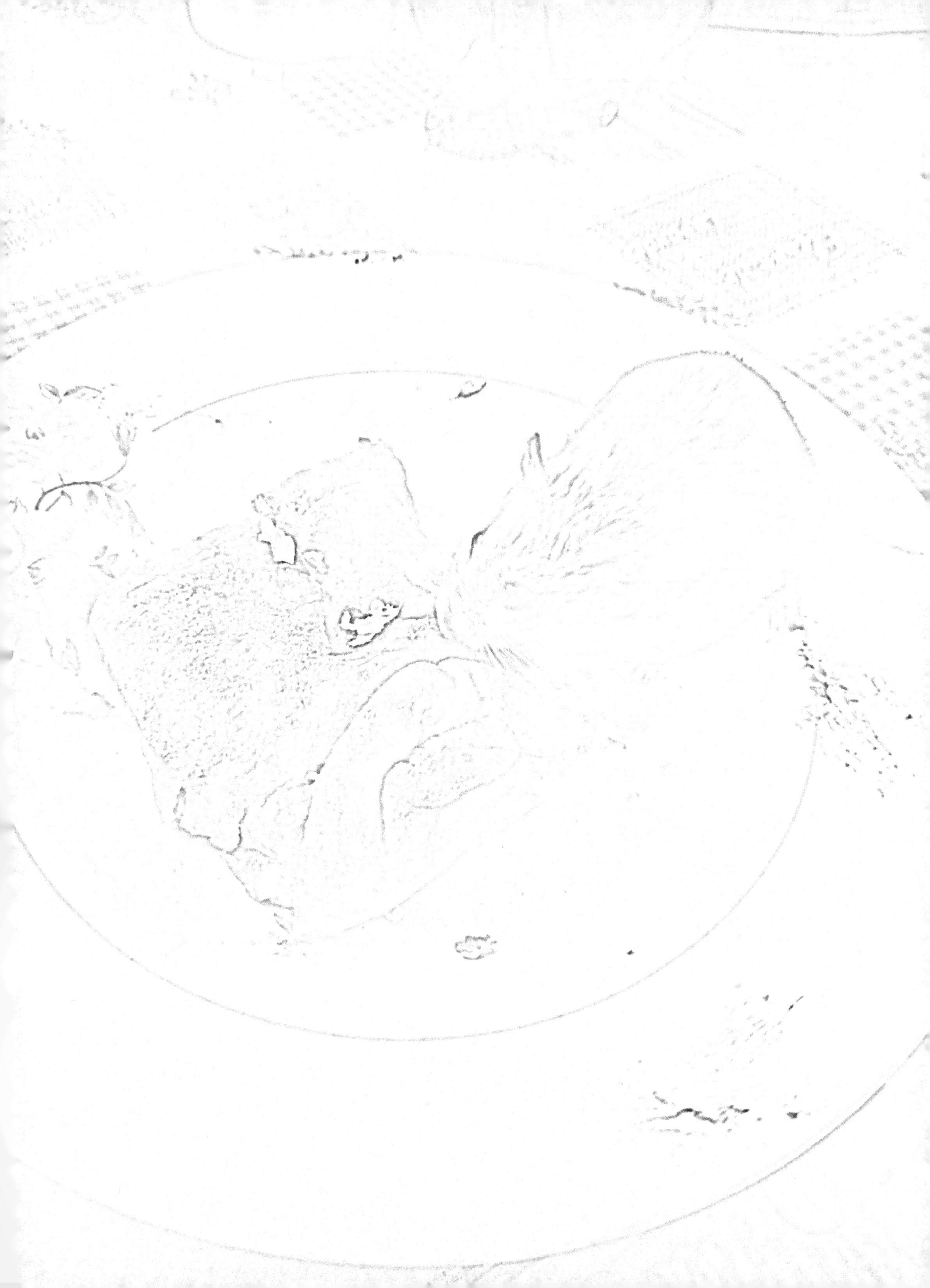

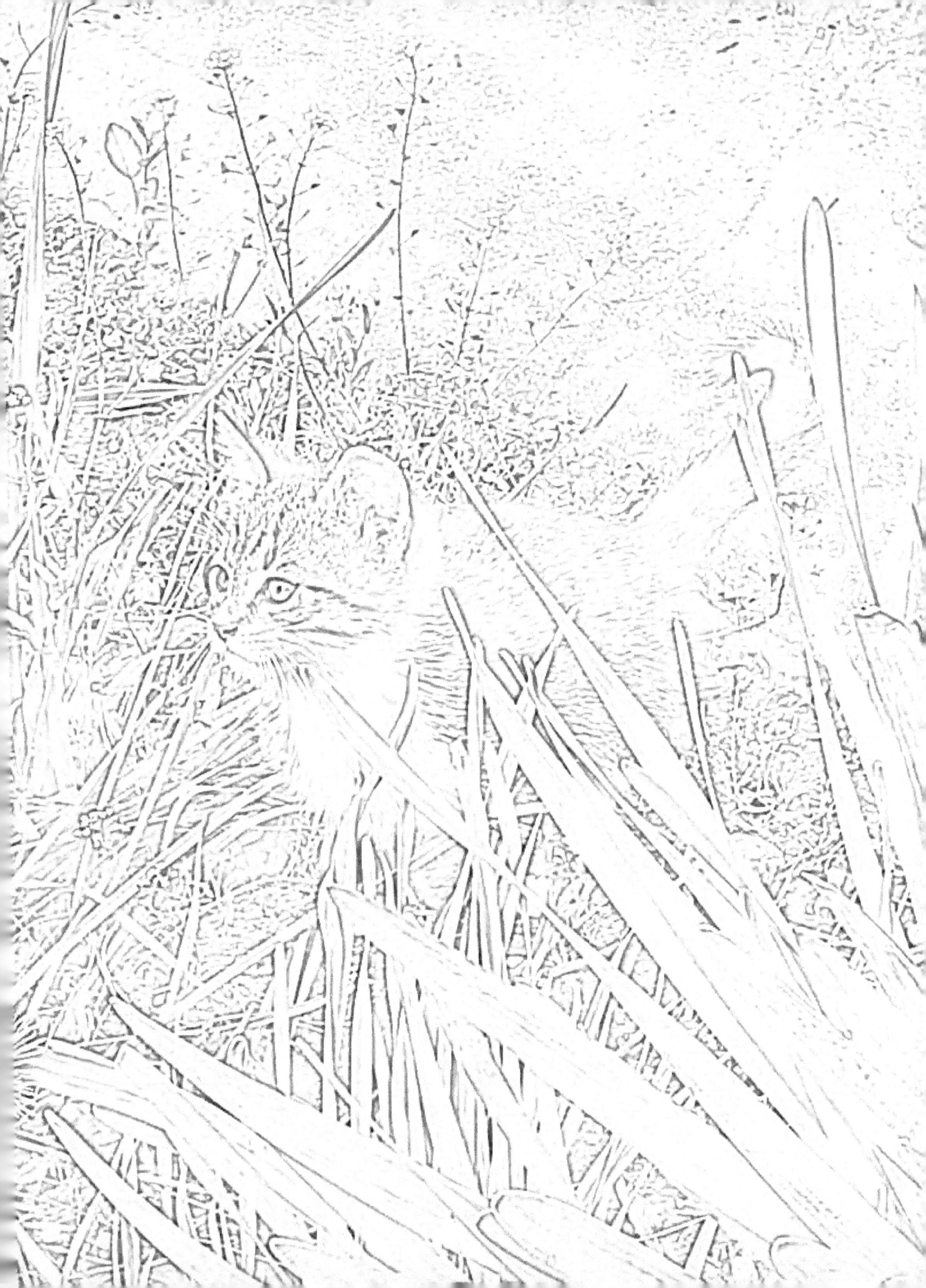

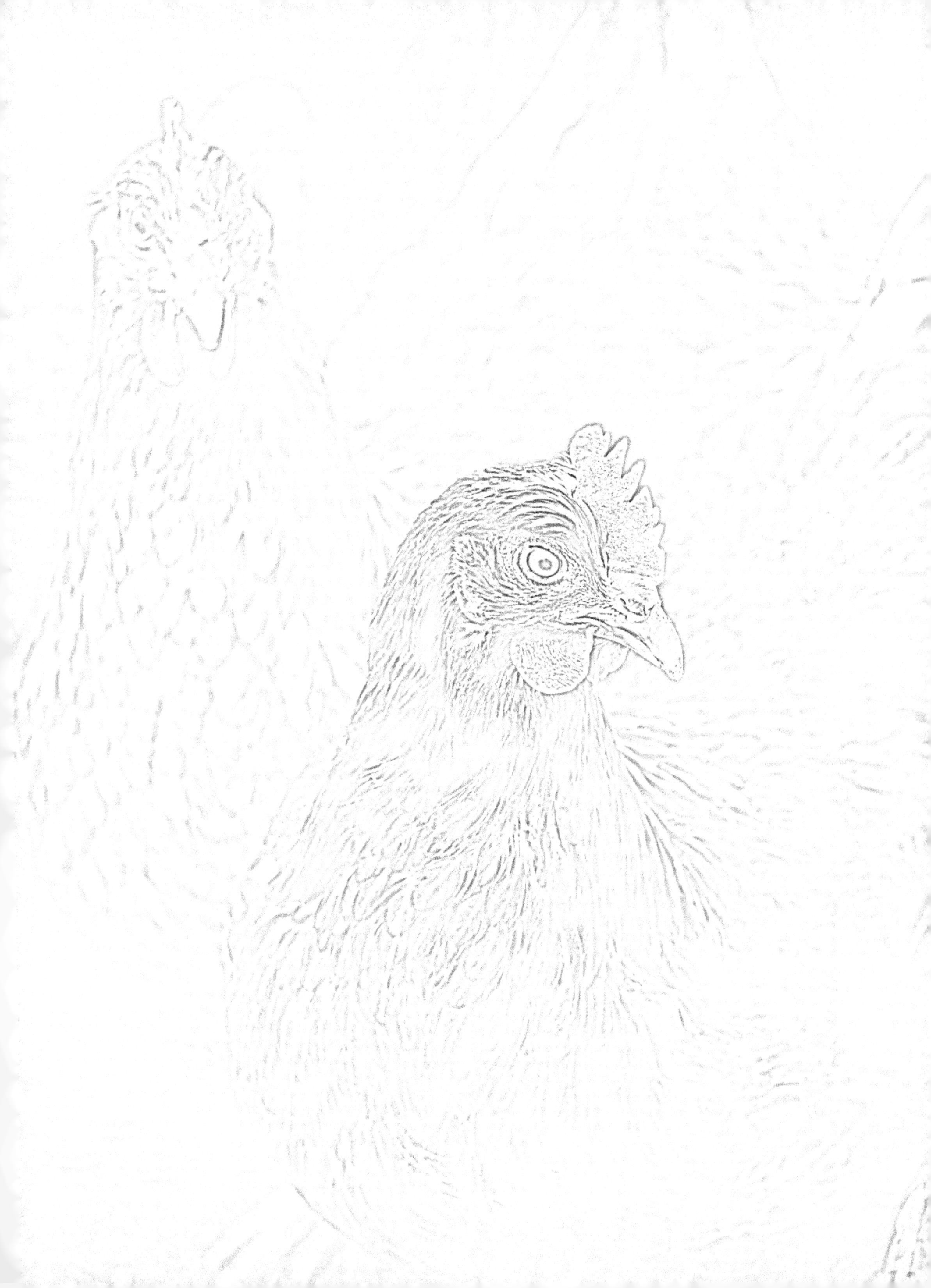

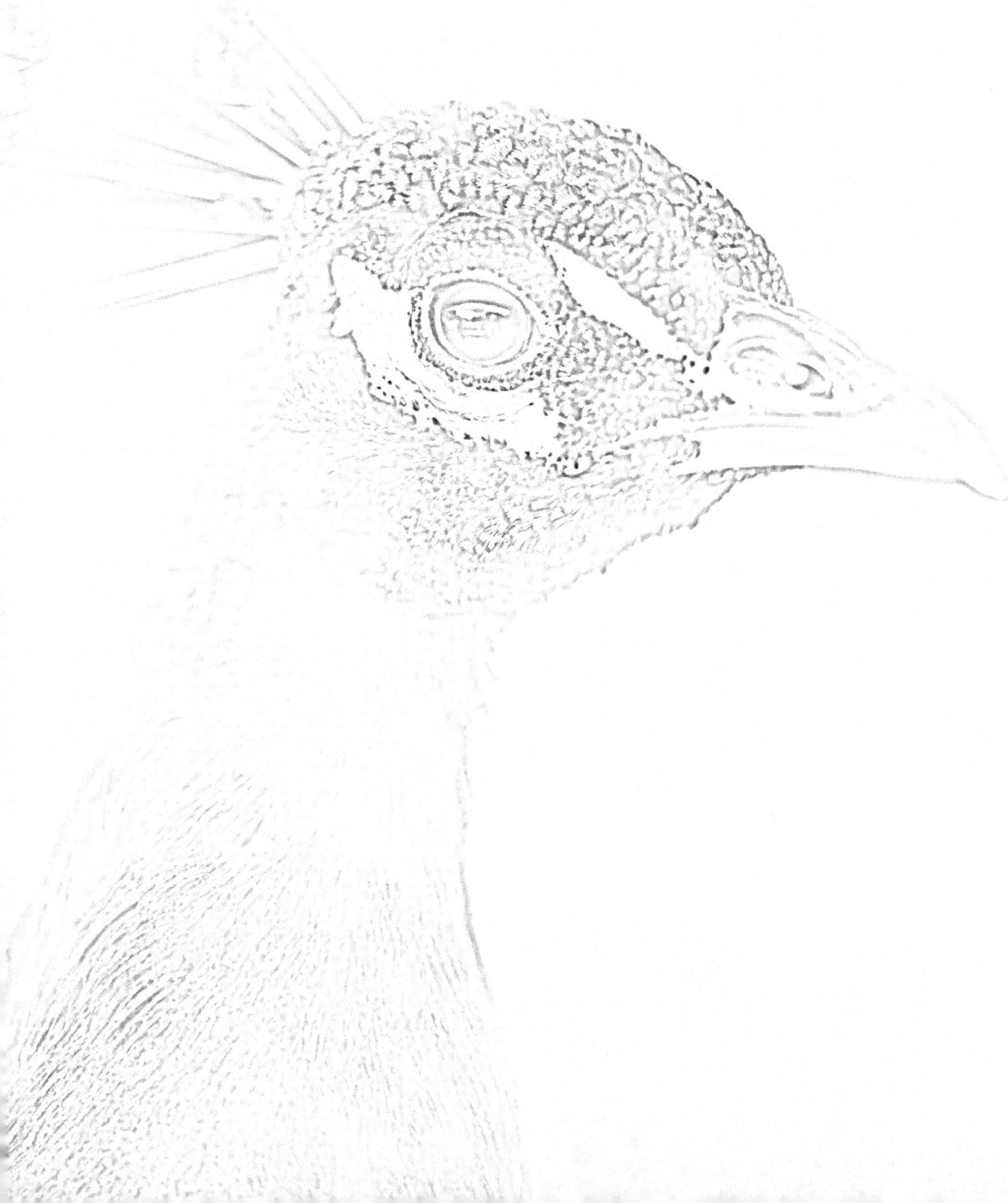

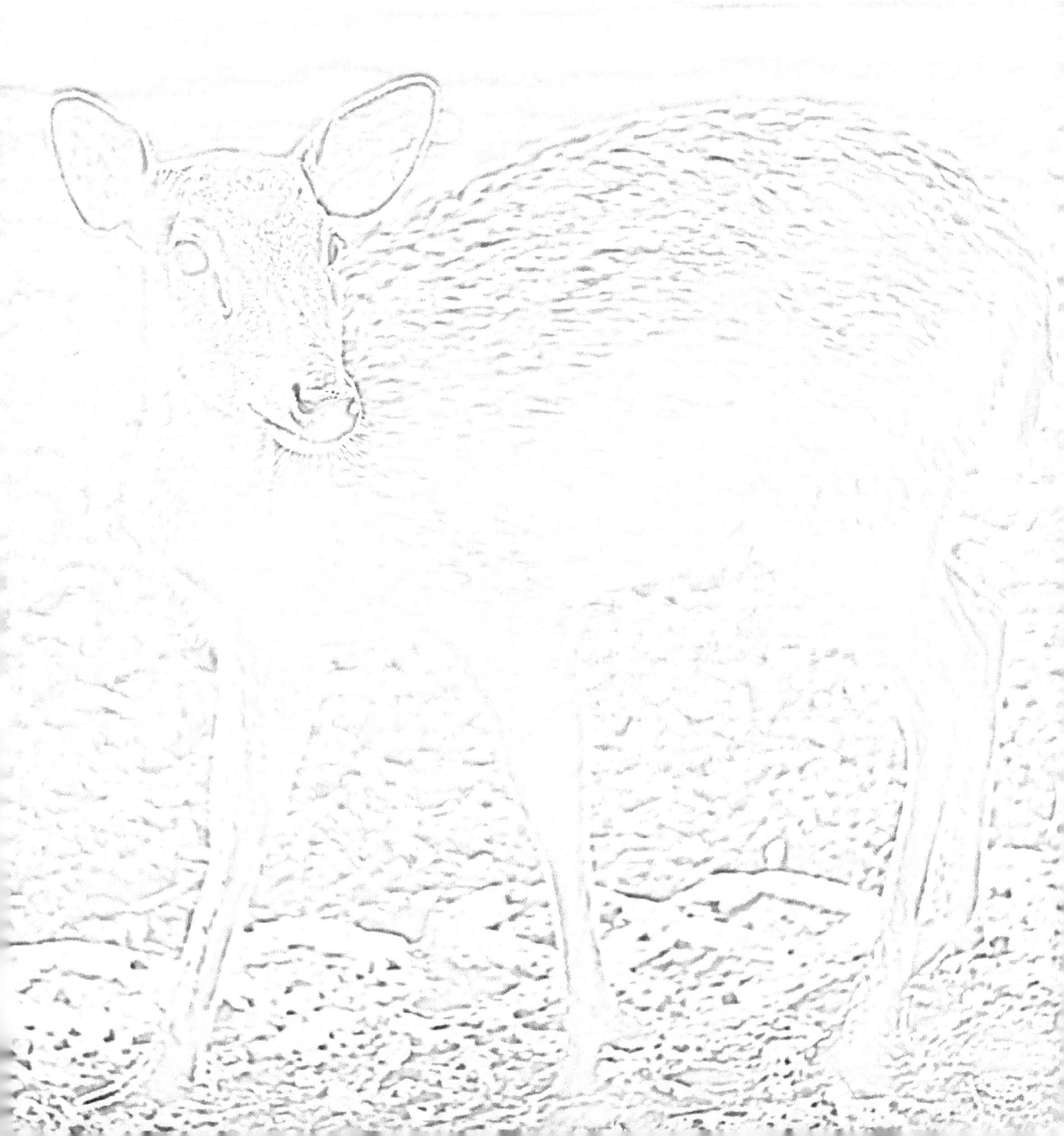

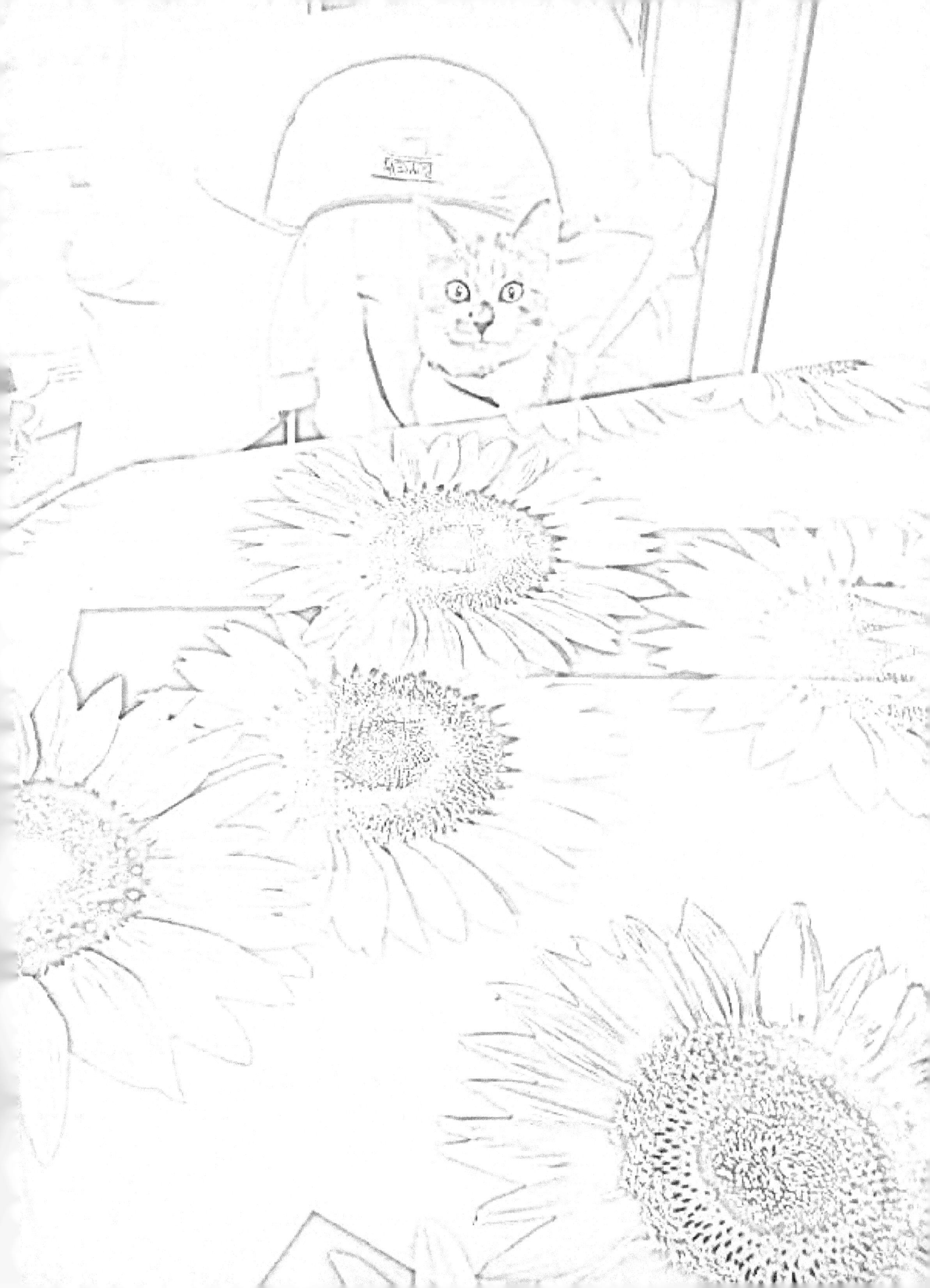

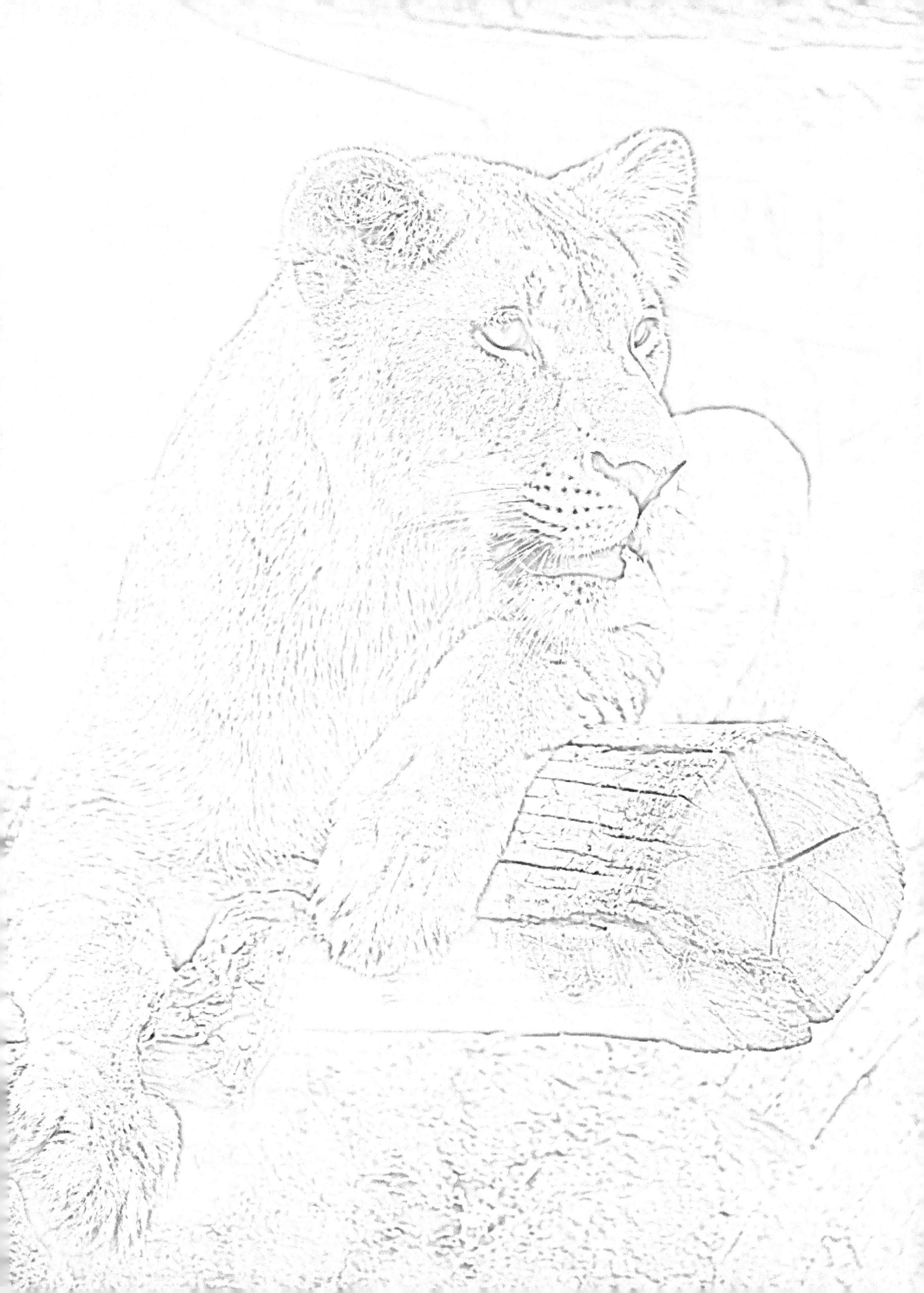

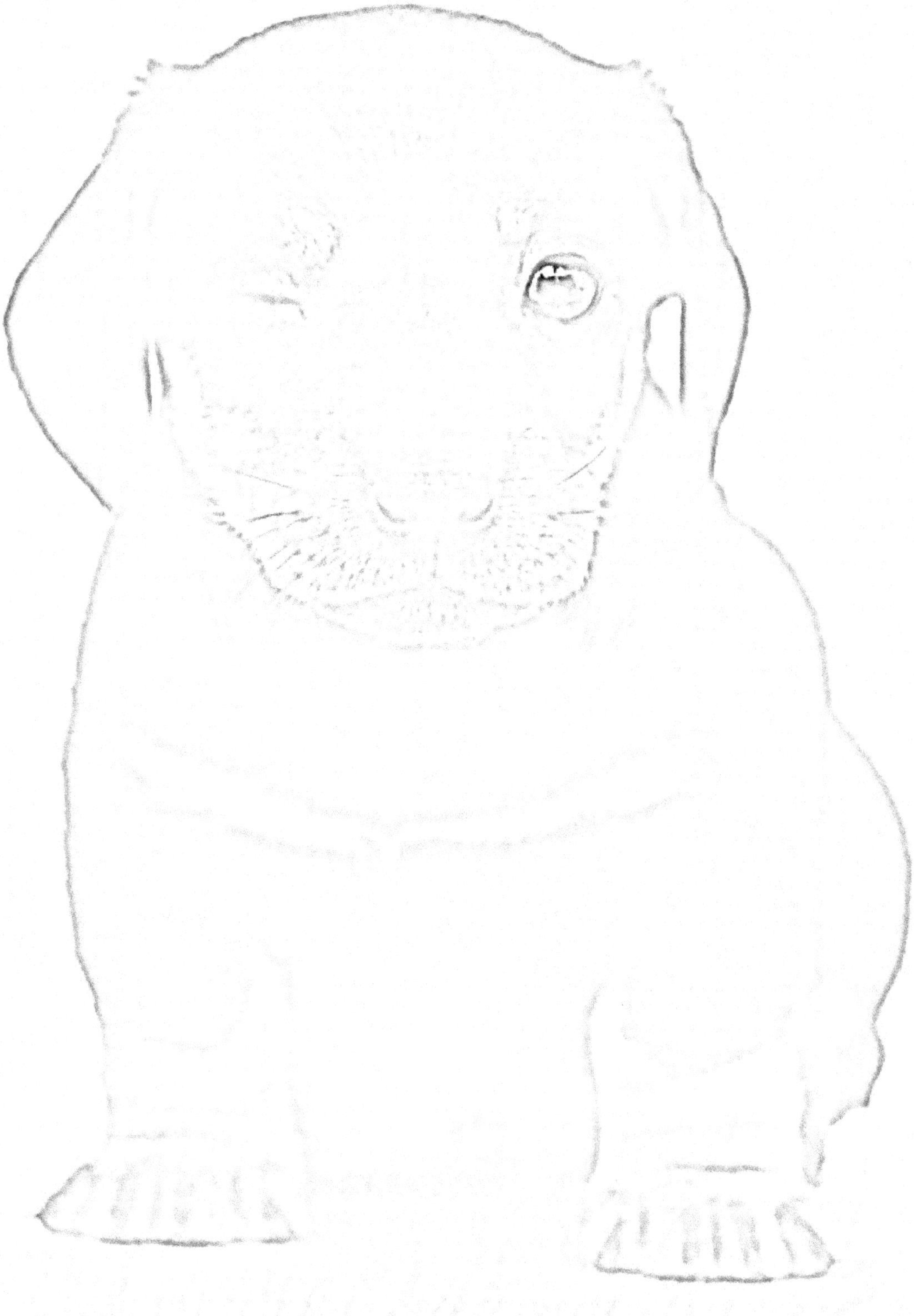

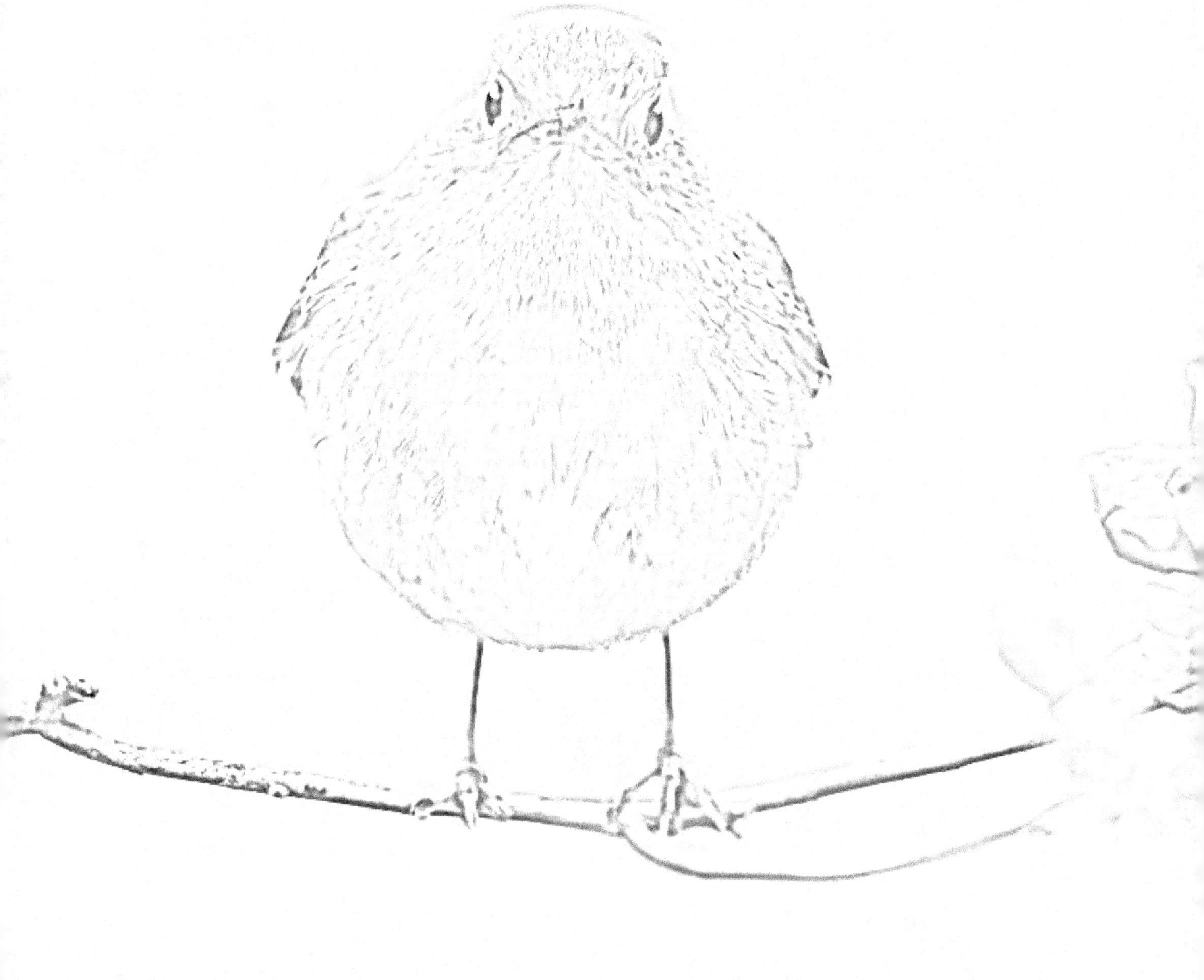

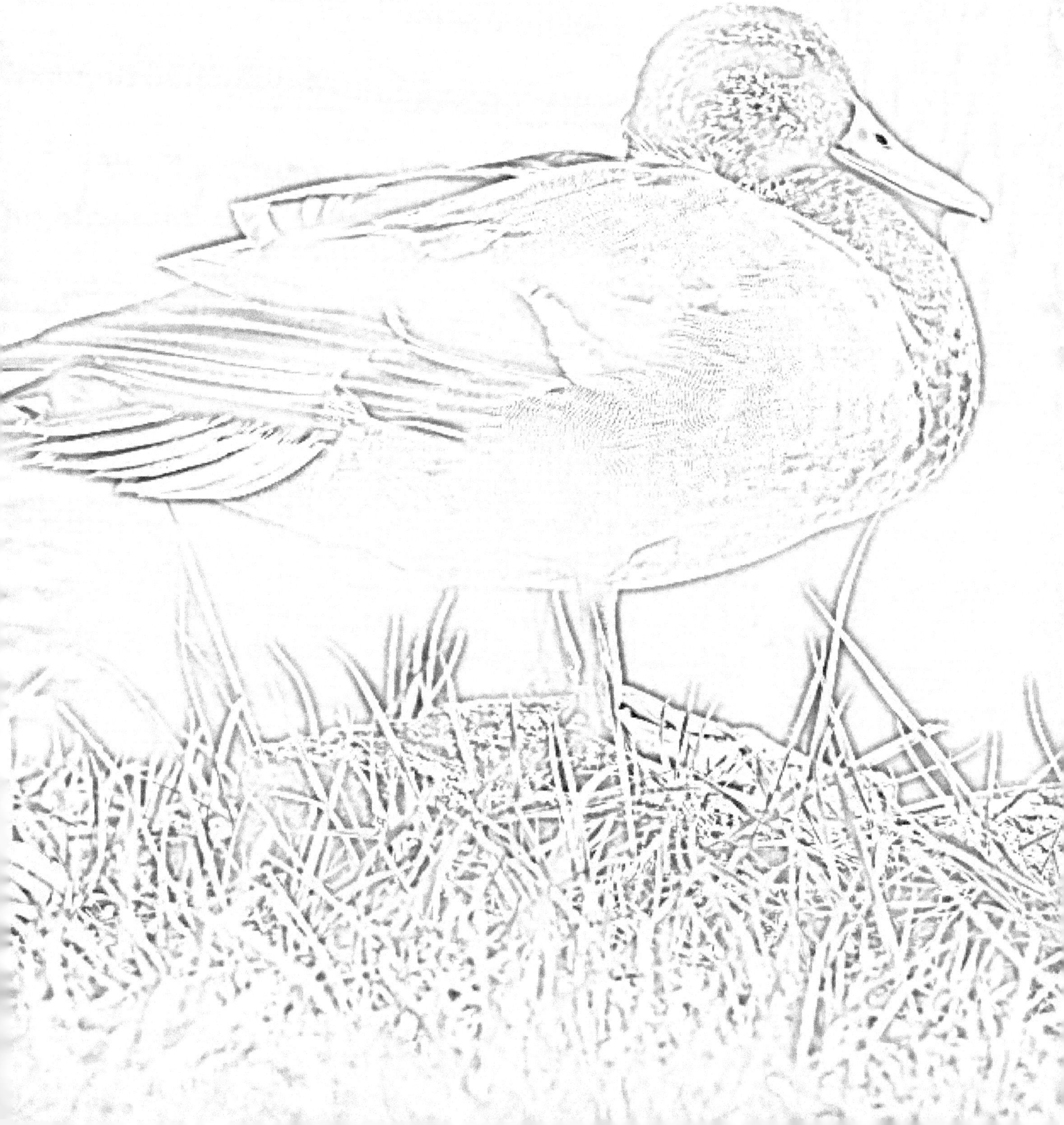

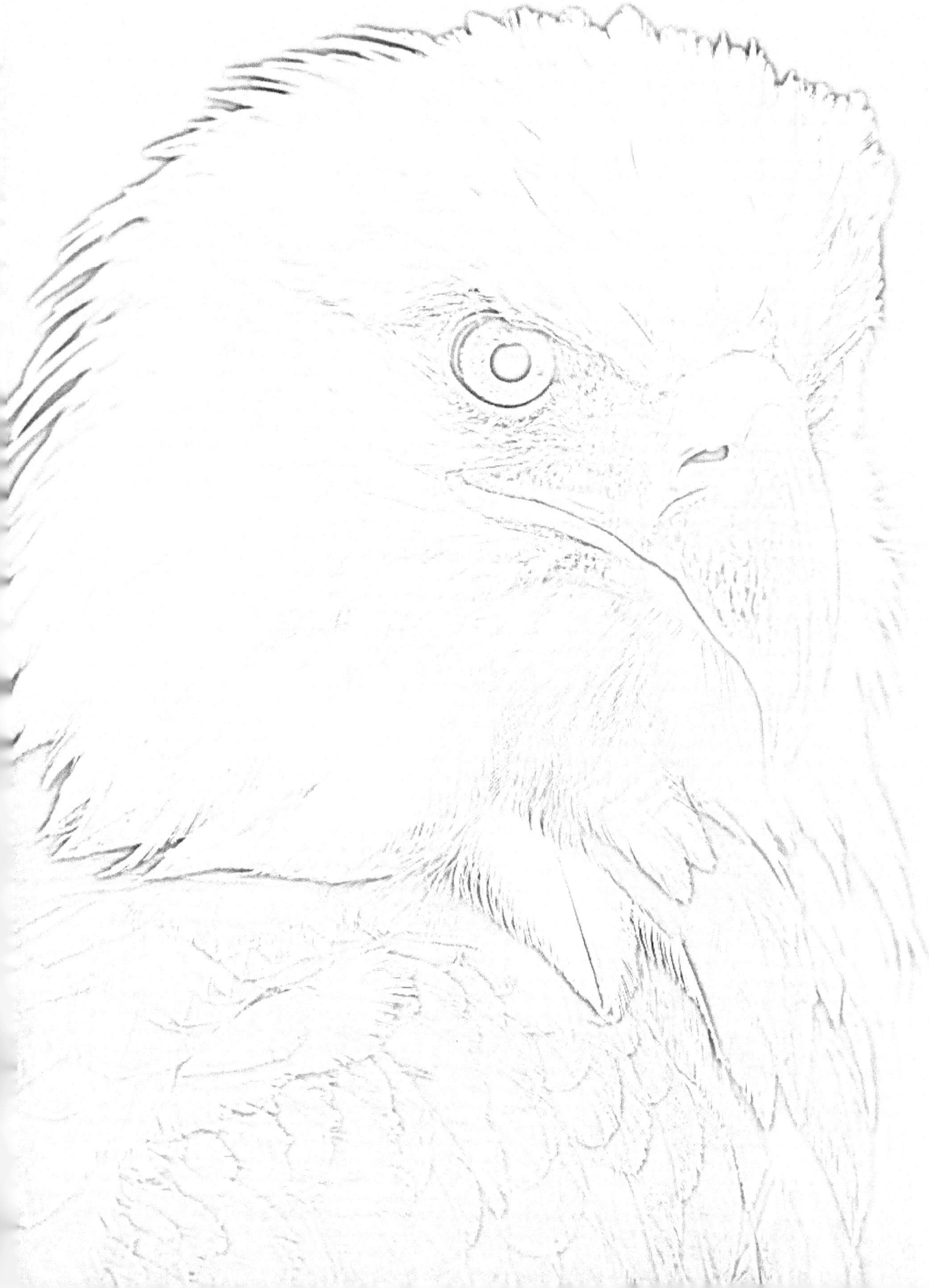

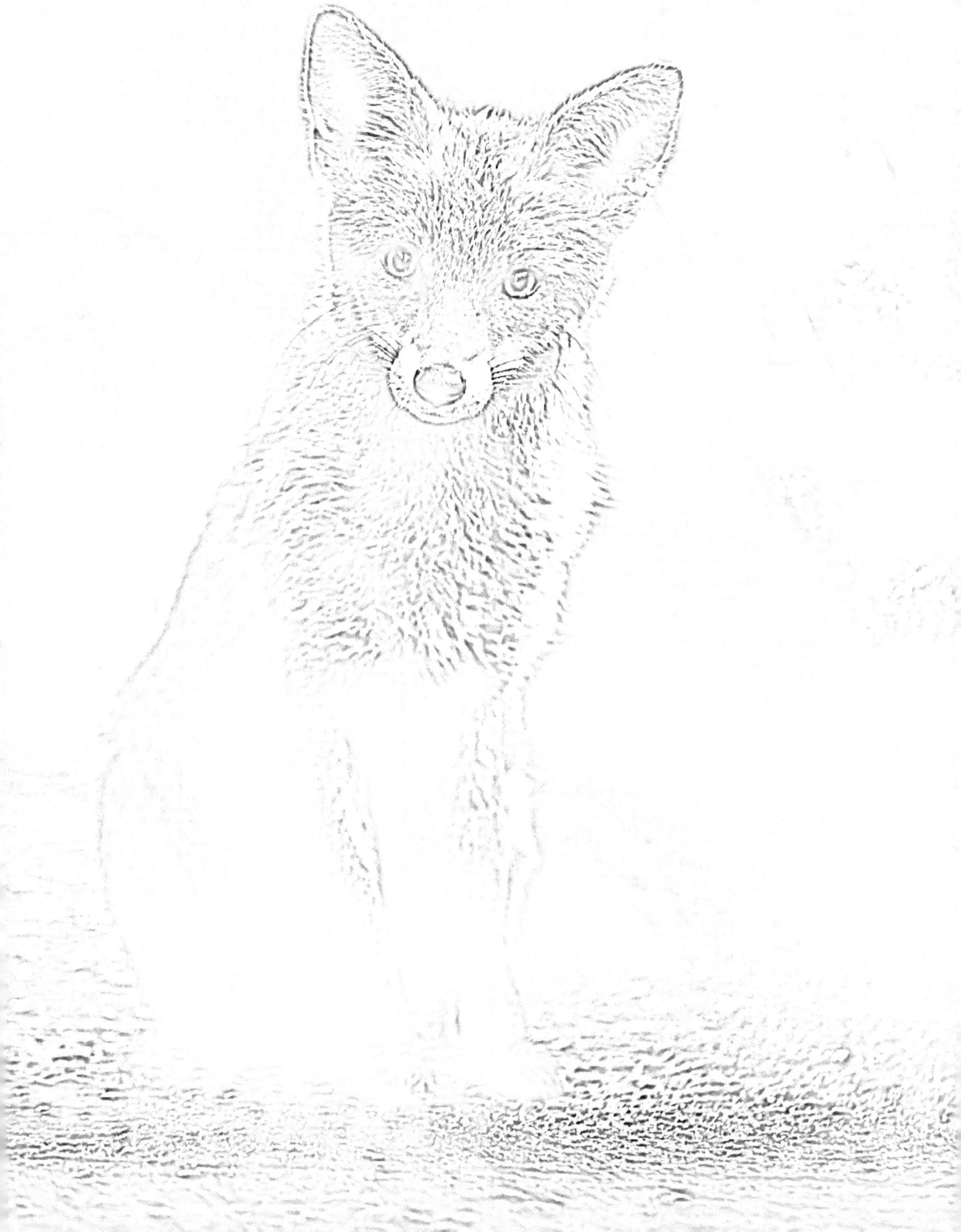

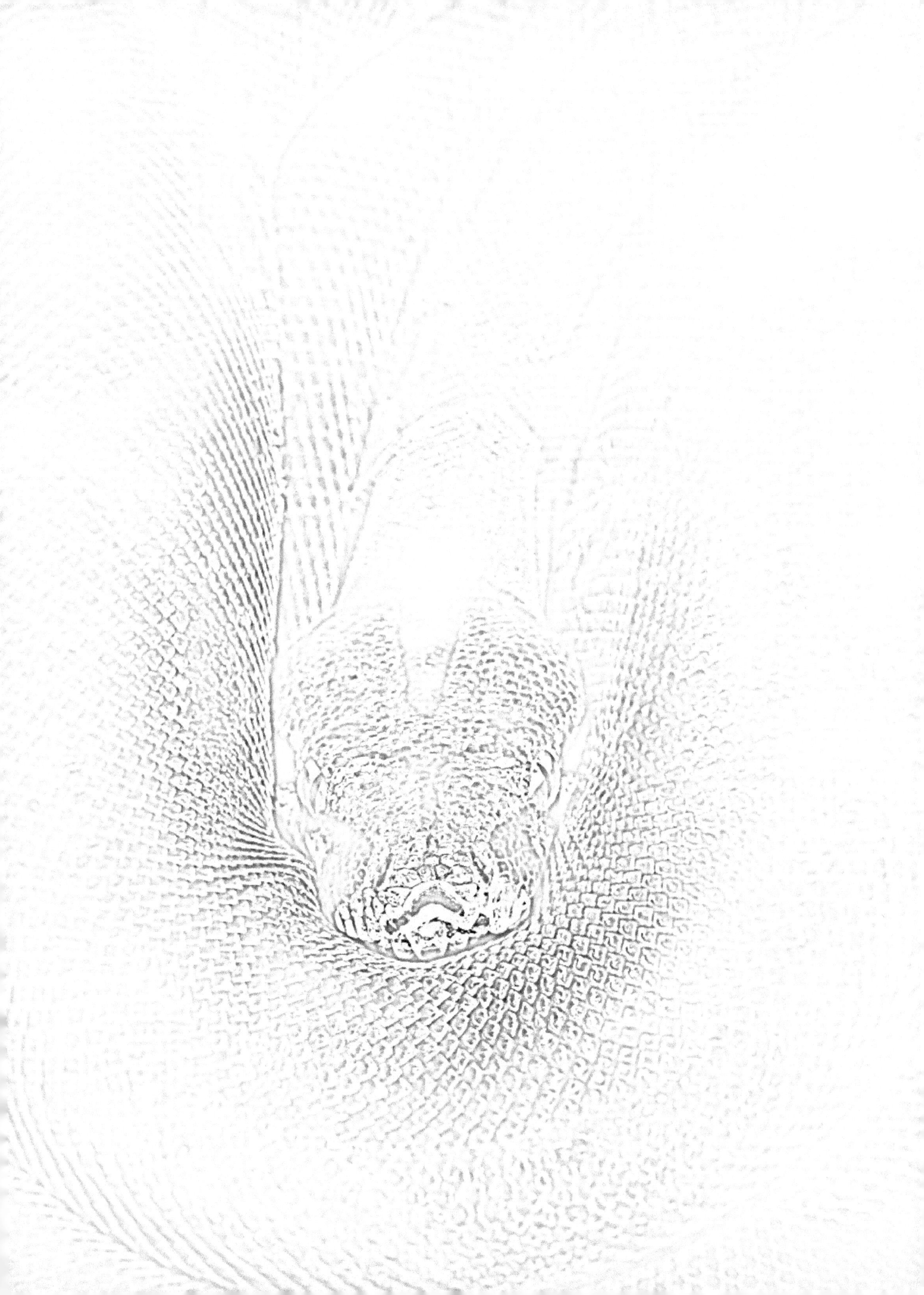

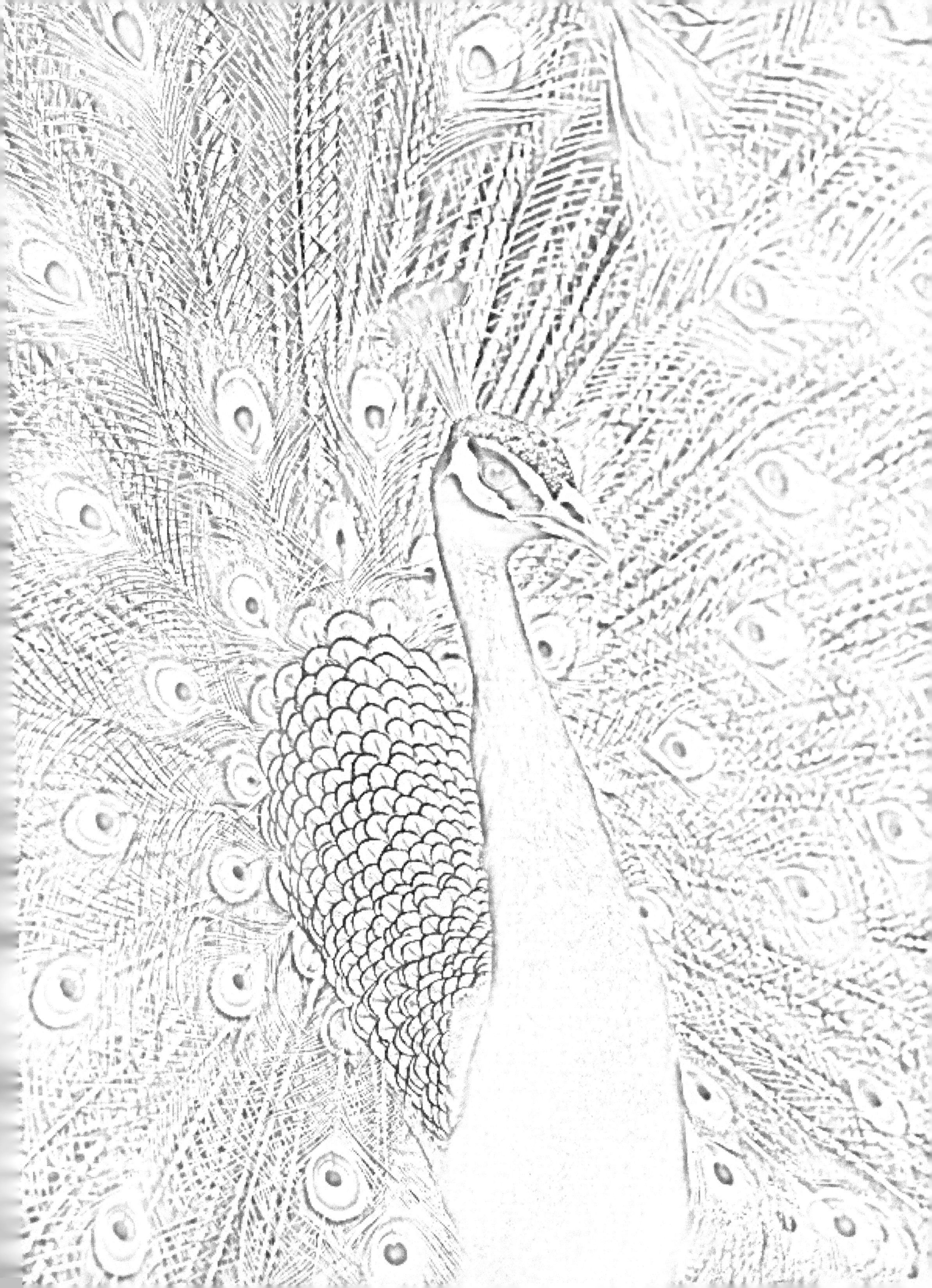

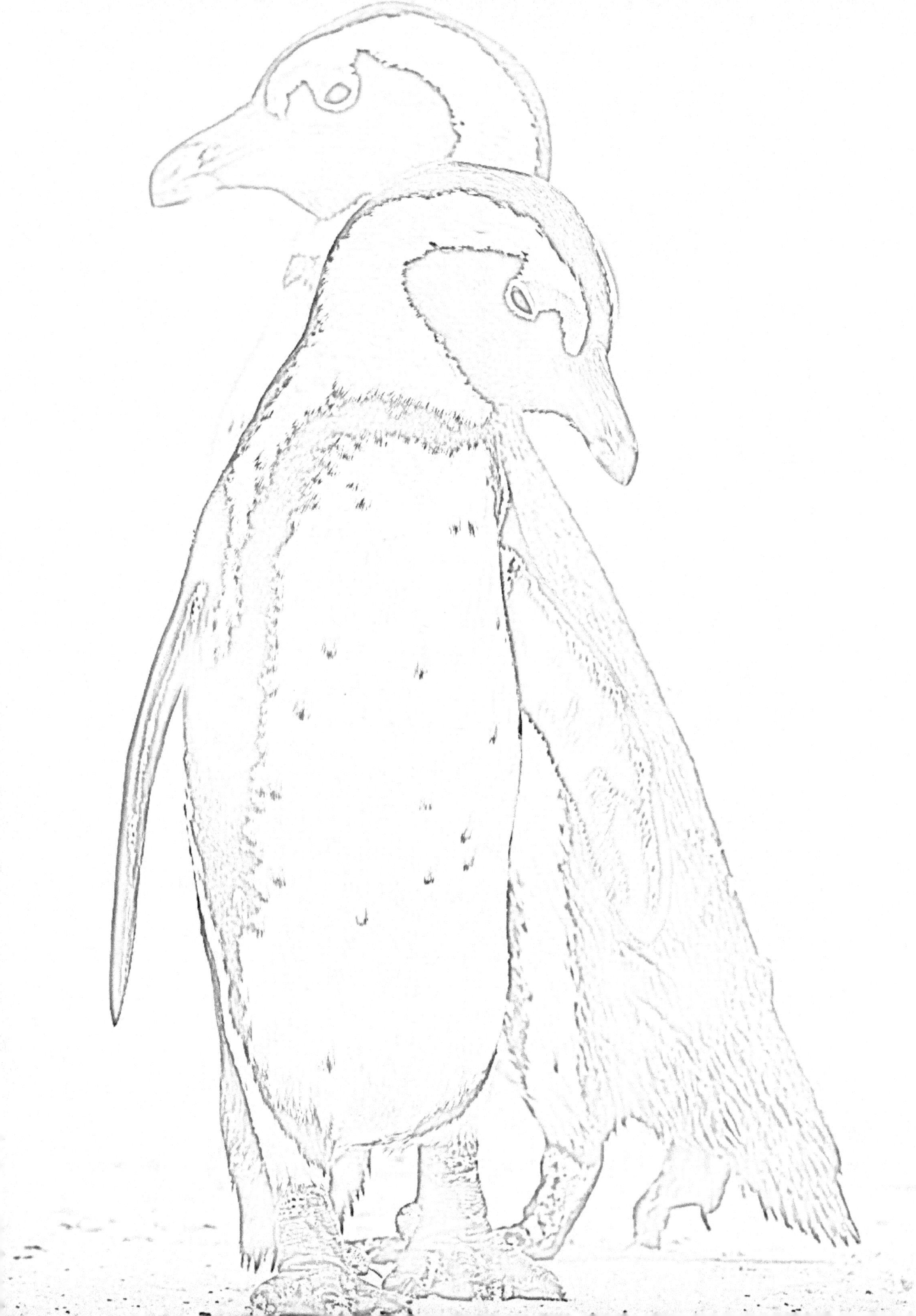

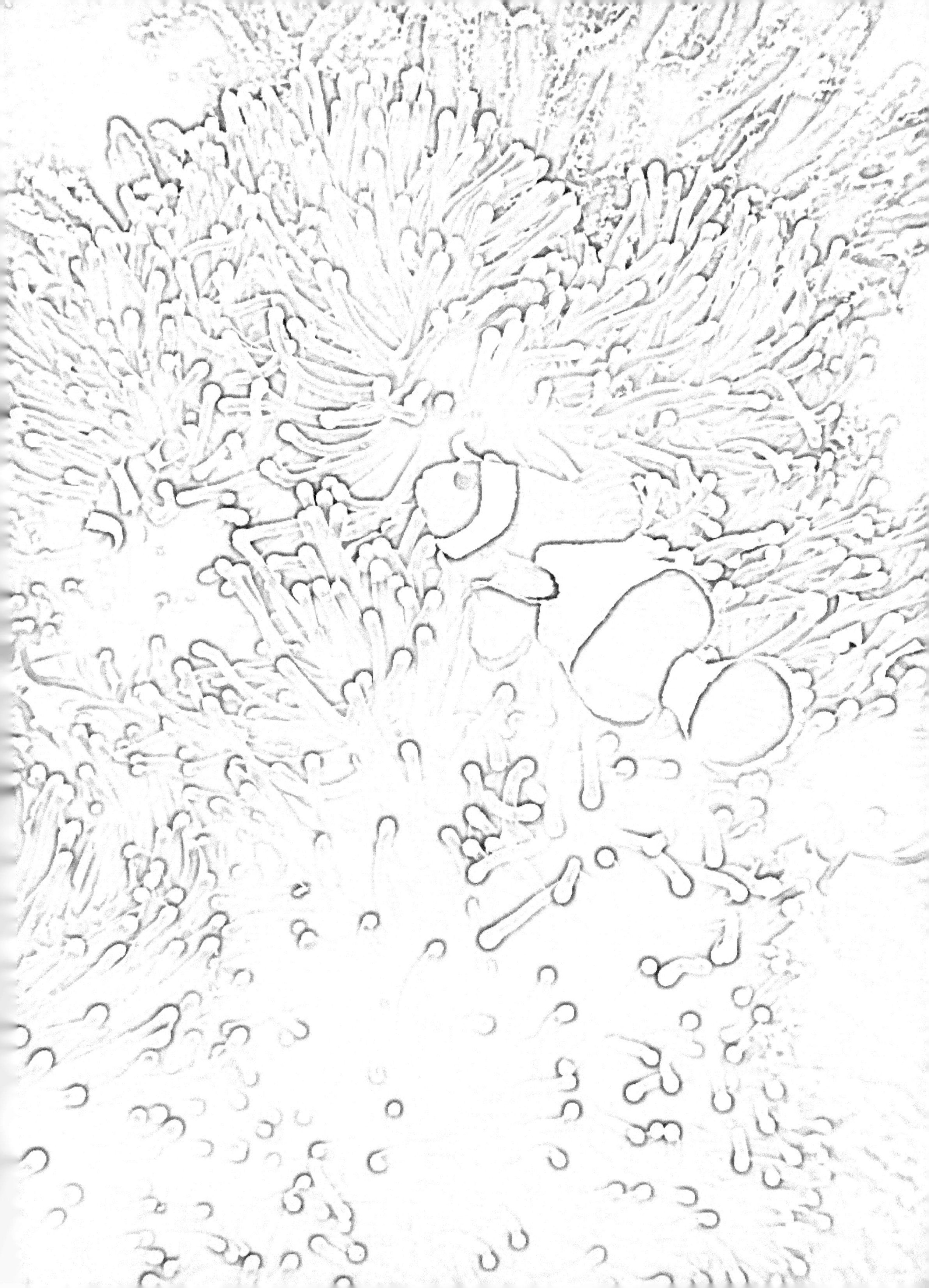

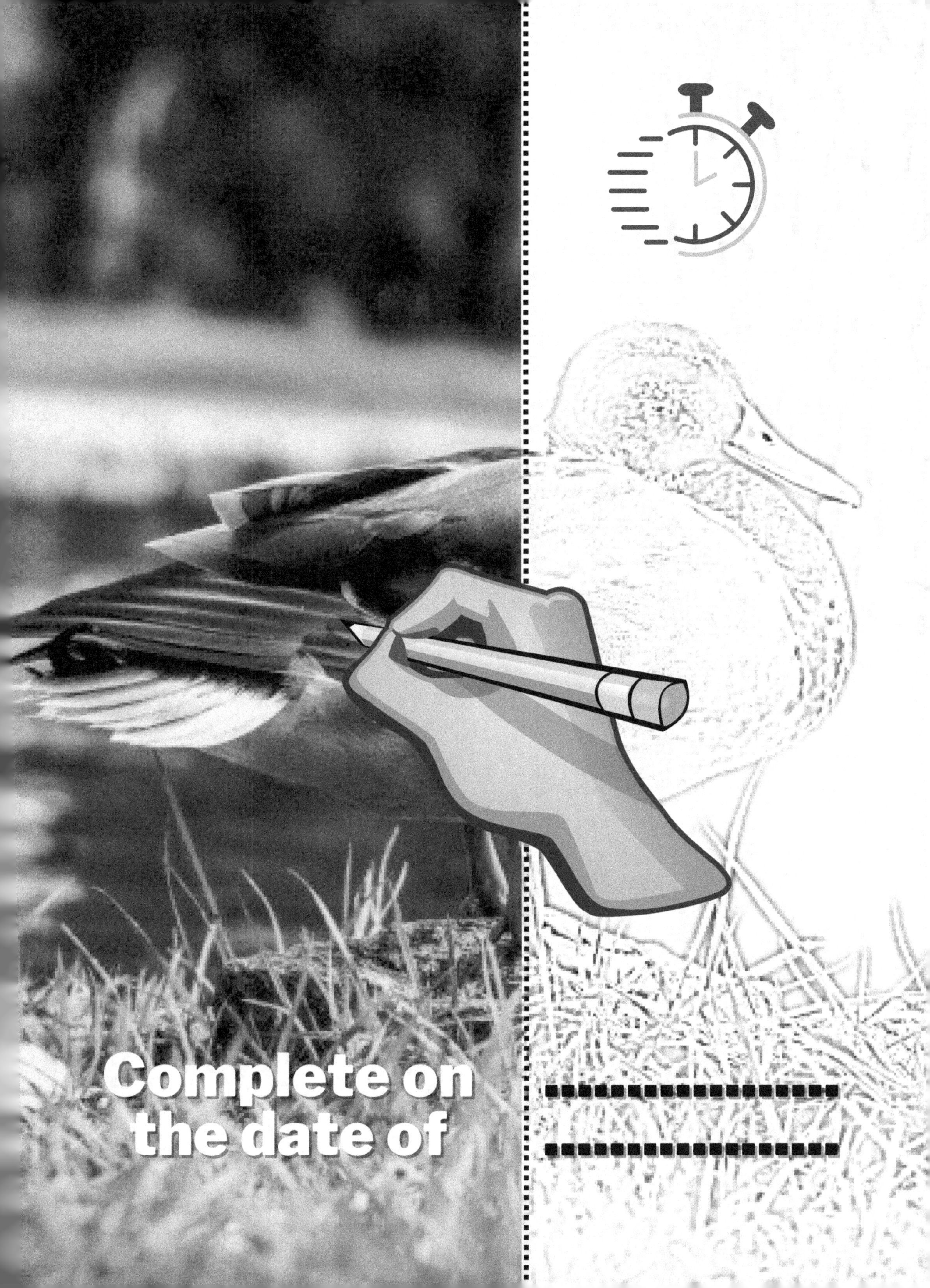
Complete on
the date of

www.ingramcontent.com/pod-product-compliance
Lightning Source LLC
Chambersburg PA
CBHW081402160726
48000CB00010B/3446
9798500470362